This book belon

If found, please contact me at:

mithmoth

Made in the USA
Coppell, TX
09 December 2019

12635476R00072